# HOW TO SURVIVE AN ANIMAL ATTACK

BY MARNE VENTURA

# The Child's World®

Published by The Child's World®
1980 Lookout Drive • Mankato, MN 56003-1705
800-599-READ • www.childsworld.com

Acknowledgments
The Child's World®: Mary Berendes, Publishing Director
Red Line Editorial: Editorial direction and production
The Design Lab: Design
Photographs ©: Scott E. Read/Shutterstock Images,
cover, 1; Paul Tessier/Shutterstock Images, 5; Chris
Parker/Design Pics/Newscom, 7; Jamen Percy/
Shutterstock Images, 9; iStockphoto, 10, 13; Warren
Goldswain/Shutterstock Images, 15; BSIP/Newscom, 17;
Mat Hayward/Shutterstock Images, 19; Matt Tunseth/
Alaska Star/AP Images, 20

ISBN 9781609731632
LCCN 2014959811

Printed in the United States of America
PA02344

## ABOUT THE AUTHOR

Marne Ventura is the
author of more than
20 books for kids. She
loves writing about
science, technology,
health, and crafts.
Marne lives with her
husband on the central
coast of California,
the home of coyotes,
deer, rattlesnakes, and
sharks.

# TABLE OF CONTENTS

CHAPTER ONE

## MOOSE ON THE LOOSE!...4

CHAPTER TWO

## SURVIVING AN ATTACK...8

CHAPTER THREE

## AFTER AN ATTACK...14

CHAPTER FOUR

## PREVENTING ATTACKS...18

GLOSSARY ... 22

TO LEARN MORE ... 23

INDEX ... 24

# MOOSE ON THE LOOSE!

It was a Thursday morning in November 2007. Hans Jorgen Olsen and his little sister took a shortcut through the woods. They were going to the school bus stop in their hometown of Leksvik, Norway. Hans did not know a moose lived in the forest. Suddenly, he saw the big animal moving quickly toward him and his sister.

Twelve-year-old Hans had learned a few survival tricks from his favorite video game. He knew that he should distract the moose. It would give his ten-year-old sister a chance to escape. Hans yelled. The moose focused on him. His sister ran away. She was safe. But the moose **charged** at Hans.

Hans turned and ran. The moose followed. It caught up to Hans and **butted** him in the back. Hans's backpack

Moose attacks are rare. Moose may be more aggressive during the mating season in the fall or in spring when they have young calves.

## THE MALARIA CYCLE

Mountain lions and sharks can be deadly, scary animals. But tiny mosquitoes cause approximately one million deaths per year. They **transmit** malaria. This is a disease caused by a one-celled **parasite**. Female mosquitoes drink blood from humans and animals. Malaria cells can move into the mosquito when it pierces the skin of an infected person. Then, when the mosquito bites another person, the cells can move into the new person's bloodstream.

softened the moose's blow. But Hans fell facedown to the ground. He rolled over. The big animal was standing over him. Hans made eye contact with the moose. Then he remembered another trick. Hans closed his eyes. He relaxed all his muscles and lay still. The **strategy** worked! The moose lost interest. It wandered away after a little while.

Once the moose was gone, Hans got up and found his sister. They made it to the bus stop and went to school. The school nurse checked Hans. He had only a few bruises from the attack.

People around the world share their living space with animals. Campers, hikers, and hunters enter the world of bears and mountain lions. Fishermen and swimmers sometimes find themselves near sharks, alligators, and crocodiles. Even people who do not go out into the woods or water come face-to-face with animals.

How can people work and play near animal **territory** without getting hurt? They can learn how animals behave and how to react. This way, they will know what to do if an animal attacks.

Many wilderness areas have signs with information about animals in the area.

# CHAPTER TWO

# SURVIVING AN ATTACK

Animal attacks are rare. Most people are not bothered or hurt by a moose, bear, mountain lion, snake, or shark. But sometimes people go into an animal's territory. And the animal feels threatened. A scared animal's instinct is often to attack. There are different ways to deal with animals that attack.

## Bears

Campers and hikers should find out ahead of time if they are entering bear country. Black and grizzly bears do not usually go near people on purpose. But they may attack if they are scared or surprised. The best defense for people near a bear is to stay calm. You can talk softly to the bear and back away slowly. If the bear still feels threatened, it might charge. You can spray the bear

A bear may click its teeth, stick out its lips, breathe loudly, or slap its paws on the ground to show that it feels threatened.

Rattlesnakes do not always rattle before they attack.

with pepper spray if this happens. You can also drop something to distract the bear. This might give you time to get away. But sometimes bears continue to follow. You can lie still, curl up in a ball, and protect your head if this happens. The bear may lose interest and leave.

## Mountain Lions

People use a different approach when mountain lions attack. You should raise your jacket up to look bigger in this case. If you are with others, everyone should stand together with their arms lifted. You can throw rocks, use pepper spray, growl, or yell to scare the animal away. You can also use a stick to poke it in the eyes or mouth.

## Snakes

Snakes are another danger for people who spend time outside. It is good to know which snakes are venomous. The United States has four types of venomous snakes. Rattlesnakes are the most common. They are easiest to spot because they have rattles on their tails. Copperheads are reddish-brown. They have an hourglass pattern on their skin. They live in the southern and

### CAMOUFLAGE

Many animals have evolved to look so much like their surroundings that they cannot be seen. In the ocean, the reef stonefish looks like a sand-covered rock. It rests in shallow water in the Indian and Pacific oceans. Stonefish stay close to the ocean floor. Prey swim by without seeing them. This makes it easy for the stonefish to get food. Over many years, stonefish with camouflage survived and reproduced. Stonefish that did not look like their surroundings were more likely to die.

eastern states. Cottonmouths can be found in or near the water. They live in the southeastern United States. Coral snakes also live in the South. Their skin features wide red and black bands and narrow yellow ones. Usually people are bitten by snakes because they get too close to the snake without seeing it. People bitten by a snake should stay calm. They should back away from it, slowly. It is important to know what kind of snake bit you. This helps doctors choose the right **medication**.

## Sharks

People in the ocean may be in danger if they go into a shark's space. Sometimes you can calmly swim away when you see a shark. Other times, you may see that a shark is about to attack. Swimmers should stab or poke the shark's eyes or gills if it attacks. Punching the shark's nose is also good. Sharks do not eat people. So a shark may swim away after it bites. Shark attacks are very rare. The chance of being attacked by a shark is one in 11.5 million!

# Alligators and Crocodiles

Alligators and crocodiles are strong and fast in the water. It is best to get out of the water if one charges toward you. Then run away quickly. These animals have short legs. Things like bushes and logs will slow them down. If an alligator or crocodile catches a person, the best defense is to poke it in the eye.

Most shark attacks occur because sharks mistake humans for prey.

# CHAPTER THREE

# AFTER AN ATTACK

People who survive an animal attack usually need help from a doctor right away. Someone can call for help. If a phone is not available, someone can stay with the hurt person while another person gets help. Other times, hurt people cannot be left alone or are far away from help. It is important to know what to do until help arrives.

People can only yell for so long before they lose their voices. Packing a whistle or air horn in your backpack is a great idea. You can use these to call for help without getting tired. Other campers, hikers, or rescue workers might hear you. And the sound will help stop a second animal attack. Sometimes people are in remote areas. They need to be seen from helicopters or planes. Signals are easy to see from the sky. Bright colors are best.

Movement can help attract attention from rescue planes and helicopters.

Mirrors that reflect the sun are also good. Hikers who can still walk can leave notes along the trail. Other hikers might find these and come to help.

It is a smart idea to travel with a first-aid kit. Learning the basic rules of first aid will come in handy after an animal attack.

People who are seriously hurt should not be moved. Movement might hurt them more. Injured people might go into **shock** shortly after they get hurt. They will look pale and feel cold but sweaty. They might feel sick and dizzy. Keep a shock victim warm and calm. Cover wounds lightly with something clean. This helps stop infection. Wrap cloth around cardboard to make a **splint** for broken bones. Then use ice or cold water to slow the swelling.

If a snake bites, it is important to know if it is venomous. Take a photo of the snake if you can. Help the victim stay calm and still. Venom travels faster when more blood moves through the body. Remove any jewelry or tight clothing near the bite. Swelling may make it hard to take off. Do not ice or wrap the bite or try to stop the bleeding. Snake venom needs fast treatment. So get help as soon as possible.

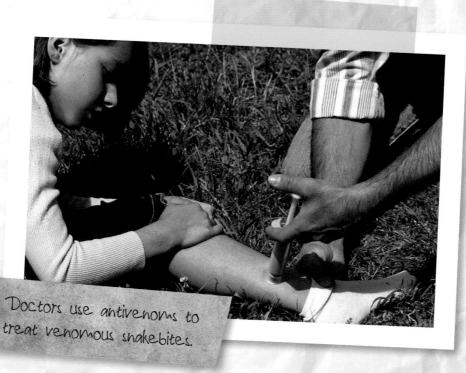

Doctors use antivenoms to treat venomous snakebites.

# CHAPTER FOUR

# PREVENTING ATTACKS

The best way to survive an animal attack is to prevent it from happening at all. Most animals are afraid of people. They want to be left alone. People should be aware of their surroundings when they are outside. This will help prevent them from surprising an animal.

Understanding animal habits is part of staying aware. Hungry animals can be dangerous. Animals like bears are often hungry. They need to eat to store up fat for winter. Keep your campsite clean if you are in an area where bears live. Bears are attracted to the smell of food. Cook food at least 100 yards (91 m) away from your campsite. Seal food tightly. Put it far away from where you will be sleeping. Even shampoo or lotion can smell good to a bear. So it is good to avoid scented products.

Brown bears can eat up to 90 pounds (41 kg) of food per day to prepare for winter.

Campers and hikers should pack carefully. They should think about what they will need to be safe. Bear spray or pepper spray can drive away an attack from a bear or mountain lion. A whistle, blow horn, and flashlight can be useful if you need to signal for help. A first-aid kit is a must.

Bear spray can make a bear's skin and eyes burn long enough for people to get away. It is best to spray a charging bear in its face.

People who look around and pay attention have the best chance of avoiding an animal attack. Steer clear of areas where you can see lots of animal tracks. Listen for animal sounds. Look around as you walk.

## INSTINCT VS. LEARNED BEHAVIOR

A mother bear with its cubs may attack if a person surprises it. Bears have an instinct to protect their young. Instinct is behavior with which the animal is born. Beavers are born knowing how to build a dam. And spiders are born knowing how to spin a web. Learned behavior is not instinctual, or natural. It comes from experience. For example, mother bears teach their cubs to find food.

Experienced campers, hikers, surfers, and swimmers know that the safest way to go is in a group. Animals are less likely to attack a group. And if an animal does attack, people in groups can count on others to help scare the animal away.

# Glossary

**butted** (BUHT-ed) Something is butted when it is hit by an animal's head or horns. A moose butted Hans in the back.

**charged** (chahrjd) An animal has charged when it has run toward someone. A moose charged at Hans.

**medication** (med-i-KAY-shuhn) Medication is something used to treat a disease. Snakebite victims need antivenom medication right away.

**parasite** (PAYR-uh-site) A parasite is an animal that depends upon another animal to live. The malaria parasite is passed by mosquitoes from one person to another.

**shock** (shahk) Shock is a medical condition where someone's blood pressure drops seriously. Shock victims may lose consciousness.

**splint** (splint) A splint is a device used to hold a broken bone in place. A hiker can make a splint from clean cardboard to hold a broken ankle.

**strategy** (STRAT-i-jee) A strategy is a plan for doing something. Playing dead is one strategy for surviving a moose attack.

**territory** (TER-i-tor-ee) A territory is an area of land that is defended by an animal. The moose was upset when Hans and his sister invaded its territory.

**transmit** (trans-MIT) To transmit is to pass or spread from one person to another. Mosquitoes transmit malaria.

# To Learn More

## BOOKS

Long, Denise. *Survivor Kid: A Practical Guide to Wilderness Survival*. Chicago: Chicago Review Press, 2011.

Stewart, Melissa. *National Geographic Readers: Deadliest Animals*. Washington DC: National Geographic Society, 2011.

Tarshis, Lauren. *I Survived: I Survived the Shark Attacks of 1916*. New York: Scholastic, 2011.

## WEB SITES

Visit our Web site for links about how to survive an animal attack:

### childsworld.com/links

Note to Parents, Teachers, and Librarians: We routinely verify our Web links to make sure they are safe and active sites. So encourage your readers to check them out!

# Index

alligator, 7, 12–13

bear, 7, 8, 10, 18, 21
broken bone, 17

camouflage, 11
camping, 6, 8, 14, 18, 20, 21
copperhead snake, 11
coral snake, 11–12
cottonmouth snake, 11
crocodile, 7, 12–13

distraction, 4, 10

first-aid kit, 16, 20

hiking, 8, 14, 16, 20, 21

instinct, 8, 21

learned behavior, 21

malaria, 6
medication, 12
moose, 4, 6, 8
mosquito, 6
mountain lion, 6, 7, 8, 10

Olsen, Hans Jorgen, 4, 6

parasite, 6
pepper spray, 8, 11, 20
poisonous, 16

rattlesnake, 11, 16

shark, 6, 7, 8, 12
shock, 16
signal, 14, 16, 20
snake, 11–12, 16, 17
splint, 17
strategy, 6
swelling, 17
swimming, 7, 12, 21

venomous, 11, 16, 17